The Way of Pilgrimage is like a new best friend! You can walk right into its welcoming presence and begin at once to find fresh truths sprouting up from ancient sources. It will become a trusted guide for those who accompany youth and young adults on their paths of meaning-making.

It promises especially satisfying moments for leaders who wish to engage others in the rhythmic paces of spiritual formation. The weekly gatherings show us how to move from deeply ingrained habits of content-based Bible study into soul-tending practices of contemplation and community that open us to transformation.

—THE REVEREND DR. DORI BAKER
Author, *Doing Girlfriend Theology: God-Talk with Young Women*
United Methodist pastor and professor of youth ministry and Christian education

As an organization completely dedicated to the art of pilgrimage, we are overjoyed with *The Way of Pilgrimage* resources. *The Way of Pilgrimage* is a comprehensive and passionate guide that brings us back to our ancient heritage of pilgrimage through modern eyes and practical application.

Utilize these resources to teach your youth God's unique design of our lives as journeys of exploration and adventure. There is no better resource available to date that prepares your teens as lifelong pilgrims.

—SHAWN SMALL
Executive director, Wonder Voyage Pilgrimages

Finally—a spiritual resource for youth and young adults with depth and meaning! Upper Room Books continues its Companions in Christ series with an insightful and creative journey for Generation Next. I love this resource!

—BO PROSSER
Coordinator for congregational life, Cooperative Baptist Fellowship

This inspiring resource meets participants wherever they are in their spiritual walk and gently moves them toward a deeper understanding of their own pilgrimage. In the context of a Christian community of travelers, participants shed light on the most unexamined corners of their souls. . . .

As an educator of secondary students, I greatly appreciate how consistently this text works to provide spiritual development activities for every kind of learner—from still meditation to verbal expression to artistic interpretations.

—JESSICA ROSENTHAL
United Methodist educator and youth helper

The Way of Pilgrimage is a wonderful doorway into the spiritual life. Like the bountiful feast that God sets before us, these volumes are full of wisdom and blessing. Those who accept the challenge to walk with Christ will benefit greatly from this guide. Its exercises are both simple and rich. At every point, the members of the group are encouraged to journey into the heart of God.

—THE REVEREND DANIEL WOLPERT
Pastor, First Presbyterian Church, Crookston, Mi⋯
Codirector, Minnesota Institute of Contem⋯

D1371842

A COMPANIONS *in Christ* Resource

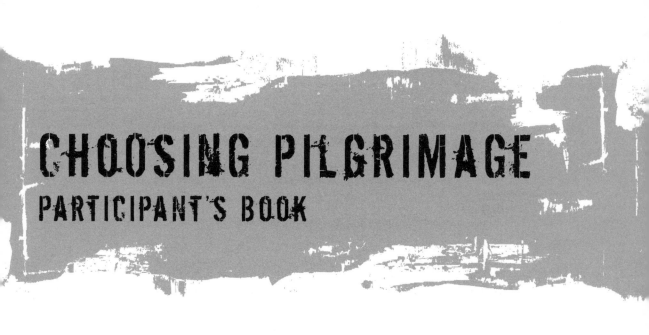

CHOOSING PILGRIMAGE
PARTICIPANT'S BOOK

Kyle Dugan and Craig Mitchell

VOLUME 1

UPPER ROOM BOOKS®
NASHVILLE

CHOOSING PILGRIMAGE
Participant's Book Volume 1
Copyright © 2007 by Upper Room Books®
All rights reserved.
The Upper Room® Web site http://www.upperroom.org

At the time of publication all Web sites referenced in this book were valid. However, due to the fluid nature of the Internet some addresses may have changed or the content may no longer be relevant.

Cover design: Left Coast Design, Portland, OR
Interior design: Gore Studio, Inc., Nashville, TN
Typesetting: PerfecType, Nashville, TN
First printing: 2007

ISBN-13   978-0-8358-9826-3
ISBN-10   0-8358-9826-1

LIBRARY OF CONGRESS CATALOGING IN PUBLICATION DATA
Dugan, Kyle.
  Choosing pilgrimage : participant's book / Kyle Dugan and Craig Mitchell.
      p. cm.—(The way of pilgrimage ; v. 1)
  Includes bibliographical references.
  1. Christian youth—Religious life. 2. Spiritual formation. I. Mitchell,
Craig. II. Dugan, Kyle. Way of pilgrimage. III. Title.
  BV4531.3.D84 2007
  263'.041—dc22   2007003688

Printed in the United States of America

CONTENTS

MEET THE WRITERS

Kyle Dugan is the executive director of Immeasurably More, a Christian nonprofit organization based in Austin, Texas. He is a graduate of Lubbock Christian University and The Upper Room Academy for Spiritual Formation. He has worked as a residential child-care worker at the Children's Home of Lubbock and was Youth Minister at the Westside Church of Christ in Beaverton, Oregon. He enjoys hiking, fly-fishing, mountain biking, and all kinds of outdoor activities. He and his wife, Marta, have a daughter, Darby, and a son, Sutton.

Craig Mitchell is lecturer in lay ministry studies at the Adelaide College of Divinity and Flinders University, South Australia. He has worked in youth ministry and Christian education for over twenty-five years at local, state, and national levels with the Uniting Church in Australia. Craig has authored numerous youth study books and articles on youth ministry. He is married and the father of three daughters.

ACKNOWLEDGMENTS

The Way of Pilgrimage is a new adventure in spiritual formation for a new generation of Companions in Christ groups. The original twenty-eight-week *Companions in Christ* resource was published by Upper Room Books in spring 2001. The ensuing Companions in Christ series has been designed to create settings in which people can respond to God's call to an ever-deepening communion and wholeness in Christ—as individuals, as members of a small group, and as part of a congregation. Building upon the Companions in Christ foundational vision, *The Way of Pilgrimage* is written for a younger audience of senior high youth and college freshmen.

The first consultation for developing *The Way of Pilgrimage* took place in Nashville in February 2005. We are deeply grateful to these consultants and to the writers of the Leader's Guide and Participant's Books: Sally Chambers, Kyle Dugan, Steve Matthews, Craig Mitchell, Jeremy Myers, Jonathon Norman, Kara Lassen Oliver, Gavin Richardson, Ciona Rouse, Jessica Rosenthal, Daniel Wolpert, and Jenny Youngman. Special thanks to Stephen Bryant, visionary leader of the Companions in Christ resources and publisher of Upper Room Ministries. All of the daily exercises found in this book were developed and written by him.

We are also indebted to those who reviewed the early manuscript and offered their insights on theology and pilgrimage: The Reverend Matthew Corkern, Christ Church Cathedral Episcopal Church in Nashville, Tennessee; Sally Chambers, St. Paul's Episcopal Church in Franklin, Tennessee; and Jeremy Myers, Augsburg College in Minneapolis, Minnesota.

The following churches and groups tested portions of early versions of *The Way of Pilgrimage*:

- Belmont United Methodist Church in Nashville, Tennessee (leader: Jessica Rosenthal)
- Wesley United Methodist Church in Coral Gables, Florida (leader: the Reverend César J. Villafaña)

- First United Methodist Church in Hendersonville, Tennessee (leader: Gavin Richardson)
- North Park University in Chicago, Illinois (leaders: Susan Braun and Jodi DeYoung)
- Milford United Methodist Church in Milford, Michigan (leader: Sherry Foster)
- Westminster Presbyterian Church in Eugene, Oregon (leaders: Jen Butler and Katie Stocks)
- St. Paul's Episcopal Church in Richmond, Virginia (leader: Steve Matthews)
- SoulFeast 2006 Youth Program in Lake Junaluska, North Carolina (leader: Ciona Rouse)

The Companions in Christ Staff Team
Upper Room Ministries

INTRODUCTION

You have made us for yourself, O Lord,
and our heart is restless till it rests in you.
                                        —Saint Augustine

We are a pilgrim people, always moving, always wanting more, never satisfied, never full and never finished. We are a pilgrim people.

Throughout the scriptures, God continually reminds us of our pilgrim hearts and calls us back to the path that leads us home. The psalmist declares, "For I am . . . a traveler passing through, as my ancestors were before me" (Psalm 39:12, NLT). And the letter to the Hebrews says it quite simply, We are "strangers and pilgrims on the earth" (11:13, NKJV). The word *pilgrim* comes from the Latin word meaning "resident alien." This world is not our home. Our life here on earth is just one stop on this all-encompassing pilgrimage, a physical and spiritual journey home to the One to whom we truly belong. We *are* a pilgrim people.

In your hands you hold the map for a six-week leg of the pilgrimage that leads us back home to God. Pilgrimage in its purest and most traditional form is not about the destination but the journey. It is not about *where* we travel but *how* we travel. Pilgrimage is a journey made on the outside to mark a journey on the inside. And as with any journey, we will need a map, a plan, and perhaps a guide. On our pilgrimage we need to know which way people in the past have gone. We need to know the rules of the road, the speed limits (and the speed traps), the curves and hills, and the construction zones. Before we begin, here are a few reminders for the road:

There is a difference between being a tourist and being a pilgrim.

Just as we can travel to holy places as a tourist, not fully engaged or fully present, we also can walk this spiritual pilgrimage of faith as a tourist. Tourists may take snapshots of places along the way and yet still keep their hearts far removed, offering empty words to those they meet. Tourists also may be here only for the community and not the journey. *This is a journey for pilgrims.*

Companions along the way are essential to pilgrimage.

Keep in mind that even though we travel with others, each pilgrim must make his or her own journey. As fellow pilgrims we journey side by side, looking out together for the One we seek.

Each weekly gathering is a stop along the way.

Each gathering is space carved out and made holy. When we gather together, the gate between God and us seems wider, and the intersection of heaven and earth more apparent. Each gathering is a place that says, *Welcome, pilgrims. Welcome to this respite. Welcome to this holy place.*

Rhythm is part of our daily routine as pilgrims.

In medieval times, pilgrims would set out on their journey in exactly the same way. Ritual and repetition were intrinsic to pilgrimage. And because pilgrims followed the same path, we can follow medieval pilgrim trails today in Europe and in the Holy Land. Every Good Friday pilgrims walk the way of the cross, the same path Jesus walked to his death (according to tradition). The repetition and rhythm of the daily exercises and readings are essential to this participant's book. So stick with them, and you will find that particular prayers, scriptures, and practices that are repeated through our journey will begin to sink from your head down to your heart; they will become as familiar and comforting as wearing a favorite old pair of shoes.

Pilgrimage is about being present in the present.

This pilgrimage is about waking up and paying attention to our lives. It also involves remembering our past. As we live our days awake to God in prayer, we will become present to God and to life.

This is a journey of the heart as well as the head.

In this journey, prayer, conversation, listening, reading, noticing, and looking are transformed from activities of the mind to practices of the heart.

You are invited to engage in the exercises each day and read the daily readings. The shaded paragraphs you'll see in the readings contain an essential idea in the passage. Be sure to get yourself a journal to use for exercises, reflections, and group meetings.

So welcome, pilgrim! May you journey faithfully and with integrity. May you make great strides, though this pilgrimage does not literally go far. As you learn to listen for the word of God, allowing it to guide you on this way, may you come to know who you really are and what you truly seek. And may Christ "dwell in your hearts through faith, as you are being rooted and grounded in love. . . . May [you] have the power to comprehend, with all the saints, what is the breadth and length and height and depth, and to know the love of Christ that surpasses knowledge, so that you may be filled with all the fullness of God" (Eph. 3:17-19).

Welcome home. Welcome to *The Way of Pilgrimage*.

—Sally Chambers
Coauthor, *The Way of Pilgrimage* Leader's Guide

We come from God, we belong to God, we go to God.

—Ignatius of Loyola (1491–1556)

This statement by Ignatius of Loyola reminds us that life is a pilgrimage from birth to death. In the exercises this week, we will be reflecting on Abram's journey from a land he was familiar with to a land he knew nothing about. In preparation for each day, take a moment to quiet yourself and open your heart to the guidance of the Holy Spirit. Give yourself the gift of fifteen minutes or so to reflect on scripture and pray. Keep a journal or blank notebook beside you to record your thoughts, questions, prayers, and images.

HEARING THE CALL

Day 1 Exercise

READ GENESIS 12:1-3.

> *Now the* LORD *said to Abram, "Go from your country and your kindred and your father's house to the land that I will show you."—Genesis 12:1*

REFLECT Abram and Sarai's pilgrimage began when they heard a call from God to start their lives over in a new place. Looking back, what have been the fresh starts in your life? Looking forward, where do you want to choose a new direction in your life? Jot down your reflections.

PRAY Substitute your name for "Abram" as you read the first few words of this verse. Sit with the possibility that "the Lord" who spoke to Abram is also trying to communicate with you.

ACT Let your shoes be a special reminder that you are embarking on a holy pilgrimage. The next time you put on your shoes today, say the prayer:

> *Christ be with me, Christ within me.*

Day 1 Reading

Dear Pilgrim,

Whoever you are and wherever you are, I can guarantee that this journey will not leave you unchanged.

The call of God is first a call to know and be known: to discover your truest and best self and to know your Creator deeply. That is what this pilgrimage is all about. It is about knowing yourself in relation to the One who paints the sunsets and cradles the sparrow, the One who inspired Mother Teresa and Martin Luther King Jr. and Bono. These people heard the second, and no less important, part of the call: to be transformed by the One who calls people to serve a hurting world—to find a worthwhile purpose beyond themselves.

In other words, the pilgrimage is about being
- shaped in the image of Christ
- by the gracious working of the Holy Spirit
- for the transformation of the world.

This is what it means to discover your truest and best self.

You may have chosen to be here, but God first chose you. Jesus says to you, as he has said to people time and time again, "Follow me."

This pilgrimage can be an excellent adventure—sometimes an extreme sport! It can take us through dark tunnels, beside quiet waterfalls, and into dry valleys—and is always a road worth traveling. Poet Robert Frost once said that he "took the road less traveled by" and that it had made the difference.[1]

Make no mistake, this is a less popular road. But it *will* make all the difference. So, take a deep breath. Look around. Gaze within. Hear the call. Welcome to the pilgrimage!

LEAVING YOUR COMFORT ZONE

Day 2 Exercise

READ GENESIS 12:1-3.

> *Now the* LORD *said to Abram, "Go from your country and your kindred and your father's house to the land that I will show you."—Genesis 12:1*

REFLECT Sometimes God challenges us, as God did Abram and Sarai, to leave what we know (our comfort zones) for the sake of a better life we have yet to realize. What are your comfort zones? Make a list of the parts of your life (country and community, friends and family, house and neighborhood) that you love the most and would have the hardest time letting go.

PRAY Thank God for all the parts of your life you listed, all the places where you are comfortable, safe, and can be yourself. Now consider: How does staying within your comfort zones keep you from following God's call? How could these comfort zones become limitations?

ACT The next time you put on your shoes and walk around, continue to pray: "Christ be with me, Christ within me." Practice awareness of the risen Lord walking with you as you go about your daily routine. Memorize the words:

> *Christ be with me, Christ within me.*

Day 2 Reading

Over the years, I have had the opportunity of visiting other countries; I have had very different experiences in each place. A lot depended on whether I traveled as a pilgrim or as a tourist.

My first overseas travel experience was a trip to Thailand, and the first place I visited after arriving was the slum area called Klong Toey. Nothing could have prepared me for the sights, sounds, and smells there. Over several weeks, I learned to relate to the local people, to say a few words in stilted Thai, to digest wonderful and weird meals, and to begin to understand the strangeness of life in this extraordinary place.

On another occasion I traveled to Singapore with a tourist group. We stayed in plush hotels where the linen was changed every day. We ate the finest cuisine. Chaperones led us on lightning tours of the main attractions. It was a completely different experience. Tourists rarely speak to a local person, other than in a gift store or perhaps a local market. Being a tourist keeps you at arm's length, detached, with a safety zone between you and the real world.

Being a pilgrim shapes experience quite differently. Our model of pilgrimage is Jesus himself—God who lived among us—who lived life humbly and simply, who ate with and befriended the poor and the marginalized in society, who embraced and loved all the world.

For a pilgrims, a single, brief mission trip is not the end of the road. Stepping outside our comfort zone to follow where Jesus leads becomes our lifelong journey.

As we travel the earth following Jesus, we must remember that we are also citizens of heaven. On earth we are strangers in a strange land. In fact, the word *pilgrim* means "stranger." If we are citizens of heaven, the world will often seem odd to us.

Our pilgrim journey is not to a faraway place or a gleaming resort but to a place outside our comfort zones, where we are truly changed, transformed into the likeness of Christ.

THE INWARD/OUTWARD JOURNEY

Day 3 Exercise

READ GENESIS 12:1-3.

Now the Lord said to Abram, "Go from your country and your kindred and your father's house to the land that I will show you."—Genesis 12:1

REFLECT God moves us forward by holding before us images of "the land that I will show you." But before we can move forward, it helps to know where we are and where we've been.

Draw the outline of a large island (as if viewing it from above) and imagine this island represents your life. Then build a picture of your route across the island as a depiction of your journey thus far. Add features (trees, caves, waterfalls, deserts, mountains, streams, sea monsters, wild creatures, rafts, or whatever) that symbolize the blessings, challenges, and experiences that have shaped you and your relationship with God along the way. For example, did a move to a new town feel like wandering in the desert? Did a mission trip feel like a mountaintop experience? Which part of the island represents your life now?

Sit back and look at the picture. Where is God in it? What would you add to represent God's call forward and the horizon of the future that God "will show you"?

PRAY Ask the Lord two questions: "What are you calling me away from?" and "What are you calling me toward?" Write what you hear or imagine as God's responses.

ACT As you are putting your shoes, think about the people you'll be with today. Pray this prayer and let Christ live in and through you toward them.

Christ be with me, Christ within me,
Christ beside me, Christ to win me.

Day 3 Reading

What kinds of journeys have shaped your life so far? Have you ever moved to another house? been on a special vacation? gone on a camp or mission trip? climbed a mountain?

It is almost impossible to undertake a significant journey without being profoundly challenged. From the time of the early church, people have chosen to become pilgrims in order to know Christ more deeply. Often they chose a special destination, a holy place, as the focus of their journey. And yet it was the journey itself, the many small steps adding together, that became the transforming experience.

To be a pilgrim means to attend to our inward journey alongside giving attention to our outward journey. We often find it easier to notice what is going on around us than to explore what is going on within us.

This pilgrimage is about being and about going. It is as much about staying attuned to the inward journey of our soul as the outward journey of our body. We must tend to the singing of our soul and to the wounds of our soul, as well as the bumps and bruises to our body.

Listen to your soul. Pay attention to the part of you that is drawn to God and the part that resists life in God. As you look ahead, ask yourself: *How do I hope to grow in the coming weeks? What aspects of my life do I seek to open to God? In what areas of my life am I seeking guidance?* You may wish to write your responses to these questions below or in the journal pages at the back of this book.

WEEK ONE

HEARING THE CALL TO PILGRIMAGE

AWARE OF GOD'S PRESENCE

Day 4 Exercise

READ GENESIS 12:1-3.

> *The LORD said to Abram, "Go . . . to the land that I will show you. . . .*
> *I will bless you . . . so that you will be a blessing."—Genesis 12:1-2*

REFLECT God's command to Abraham is joined with a promise of blessing. And with this blessing comes the responsibility to share it with others. Make a list of all the ways God has blessed you. Then think about what it means that you are blessed "so that you will be a blessing."

PRAY In prayer, let the Lord show you where or for whom you are called to be a blessing today.

ACT As you put on your shoes today, pray the prayer below. Seek to be God's blessing to someone whom God wants to bless today.

> *Christ be with me, Christ within me,*
> *Christ beside me, Christ to win me,*
> *Christ behind me, Christ before me,*
> *Christ to comfort me and restore me.*

Day 4 Reading

Luke 24:13-35 tells the story of two people who were walking a dusty road, asking why. Why had their teacher been crucified? Everything had been going so well. What in God's name was going on?

A stranger came alongside these two on the road to a town called Emmaus. He listened to their grieving. He heard their longing. Then, as they proceeded along side by side, he offered compassion and insight. The travelers came to see the tragedy in a new light. They began to realize that God was somehow present, even through these terrible events. Later, when they stopped for a meal, bread was broken, and the pilgrims recognized that their companion was the Christ. God had met them in their grief.

One thing makes all the difference to the pilgrim journey: we travel with Christ as our goal and Christ as our companion.

While I long to be with Christ at the end of my days, knowing he is with me here and now makes the pilgrimage possible and worthwhile. The same Jesus who called fishermen and serving women to follow him is the risen Christ who also calls us to the pilgrimage.

You are reading this because in some way, you have said yes to his invitation. Do you know, deep down, that he walks with you each day? Are you sure that, whether you feel it or not, he is present with you in every situation? He is. He truly is.

Christ has already come near to us, just as he did on the Emmaus road. Like those two travelers, we often fail to recognize him. We fear that he is distant, when in fact our hearts and minds simply need to be opened to his intimate presence. Much of this pilgrimage involves learning to pay attention to the One who is already with us. Christ sheds light on the inner landscape of our soul. He meets us in the people and situations that we face daily.

Today I encourage you to know that Christ is present with you, because he is your eternal friend. Seek his presence. Ask for his leading. Be open to his guiding.

MOVING TO THE BEAT OF A DIFFERENT DRUM

Day 5 Exercise

READ GENESIS 12:1-3.

The LORD said to Abram, "Go . . . to the land that I will show you. . . . I will bless you…so that you will be a blessing. . . . and in you all the families of the earth shall be blessed."—Genesis 12:1-3

REFLECT Being a spiritual pilgrim means moving to the beat of a different drum than most of the world around you. Draw two columns. In the first, write words and phrases that reflect how you feel when you move to the beat of the crowd around you. In the second, write what it feels like to be off the beat and out of sync. Now imagine that the beat is Christ within you. How can you get in touch with and follow that beat?

PRAY Ask the Lord to show you one way of being a blessing to other members of your group. Write a prayer for them.

ACT As a way of honoring God's call, decide on one little action you can take today to be a blessing to someone who came to mind as you prayed. Conclude by praying this portion of the Prayer of Saint Patrick. Post a copy of this prayer in a place where you will see it and pause to pray from time to time.

Christ be with me, Christ within me,
Christ behind me, Christ before me,
Christ beside me, Christ to win me,
Christ to comfort and restore me,
Christ beneath me, Christ above me,
Christ in quiet, Christ in danger,
Christ in hearts of all that love me,
Christ in mouth of friend and stranger.[2]

Day 5 Reading

Pilgrimage is a long journey made up of small steps. A strong tree takes years to grow. A stunning rock formation results from years of shaping by wind and rain. In a world that often pushes us to live at a frantic pace, we pilgrims are seeking to live by an alternative rhythm, to walk to the beat of a different drum.

We live in a commercial world that bombards us with messages of instant gratification. Buy now! Enjoy now! Just do it! Society trains us to expect quick solutions. Type a request into the search engine and get 127,000 instant results!

The pilgrim journey involves learning to slow down, to pause and reflect, to be less influenced by the ups and downs of your daily routine. To walk to the beat of a different drum.

This six-week pilgrimage may be for you the beginning of some new habits—habits of the soul. At first they may seem novel, then before long they might seem tedious. We encourage you to persist with them, even when you don't see the point. And don't be fooled into thinking that because we are slowing down at times, the journey will be boring. Nothing could be further from the truth.

In C. S. Lewis's book *The Lion, the Witch and the Wardrobe*, some children in the land of Narnia are being led to Aslan, Narnia's great leader. On discovering that Aslan is not a person but a lion, the children feel some apprehension.

"Then he isn't safe?" said Lucy.
"Safe?" said Mr. Beaver; "don't you hear what Mrs. Beaver tells you? Who said anything about safe? 'Course he isn't safe. But he's good."[3]

God is good, but not predictable. God won't fit in your back pocket. Our Creator is much bigger than your hopes or expectations. The Holy One is not a vending machine who will pop out the solutions to your problems. God is much wiser than that. The Lord of All can seem like a warm blanket and also a searing fire. God can seem like a safe haven and also a raging river. Don't expect your pilgrimage with Christ to be predictable, or even safe. The way is risky, and it is good. Incredibly good.

A WORD ABOUT THE WEEK

This week we retrace Jesus' journey from being named the Beloved by God in baptism to the wilderness of having his very identity and purpose questioned. Keep your heart open to what God might be naming you. As you do the daily exercises, keep your journal close by to record your thoughts.

BEGINNING WITH BLESSING

Day 1 Exercise

READ MARK 1:9-11.

And a voice came from heaven, "You are my Son, the Beloved; with you I am well pleased."—Mark 1:11

REFLECT At his baptism, Jesus hears God naming him the Beloved. When or where have you ever heard or felt you are loved with an unconditional, eternal love? Who are the people whose voices or actions have communicated such love to you? Record your memories.

PRAY Close your eyes, take a deep breath, and imagine Jesus hearing these words from heaven: "You are my Son, the Beloved; with you I am well pleased." Now listen to what Jesus wants *you* to hear for yourself through him and his story. Write what comes to you.

ACT Stick this blessing, similar to what Jesus heard, on your mirror: "You are my child, the beloved; with you I am well pleased." Each day this week pray this blessing for others who need to know they are loved by God.

Day 1 Reading

Last week you began an important journey, a pilgrimage that will take you to new places in your relationship with God and change the way you live as a disciple of Jesus Christ. You have started to pay attention to your spiritual life in a fresh way. Also, you have begun to look around you each day and ask, "Where is God in all this?" Hopefully you are enjoying the travel so far.

Jesus called disciples to travel with him. But what about his own call? Jesus' own life and ministry was a pilgrimage of love and service. How did his journey begin? Let's turn back time . . . (see Luke 3 and Matthew 3).

A wild-looking man stands waist-deep in water, yelling at people on the river bank. "Change! All of you need to change!" Some shake their heads in bewilderment. Others step forward, eager to hear more. Then John, the river prophet, stops his ranting mid-speech. A newcomer stands on the bank, waiting. John wades to the shallows and falls on his knees. "You come to me? It is I who should be baptized by you!"

Jesus enters the water and at John's hand is plunged beneath its murky surface. A strong arm holds him under. This is more than a dip; it seems like a drowning. Then he rises—gasping, dripping, eyes wide, pulse racing. Jesus opens his mouth as if to speak. Suddenly a brightness splits the sky. It is as if the heavens themselves open, and the Spirit swoops down like a bird to claim him. A voice speaks forth with meaning beyond words to those gathered, "This is my Son, the Beloved, with whom I am well pleased."

Only when Jesus hears and knows that he is deeply beloved by God and deeply pleasing to God can he begin his pilgrimage of ministry. At the start of this journey, Jesus does not receive a command or decree from God; instead he receives a blessing. Jesus does not receive a map or itinerary from God; instead he receives a calling.

The Christian spiritual journey is grounded in baptism, a sure sign that our identity resides in God's love and that faith is a gift from God. When you are baptized, and as you live out your baptism, God says to you, "You are my beloved. With you I am well pleased." This is true for you because it was first true for Jesus.

God's goodness, not our own, is the source of blessing. And your baptism, like Jesus' own, is a mark of your calling to trust, follow, and serve.

DEEPENING IDENTITY THROUGH TESTING

Day 2 Exercise

READ LUKE 3:21-22; 4:1-13.

> *Jesus . . . was led by the Spirit in the wilderness, where for forty days he was tempted. . . . The devil said to him . . .—Luke 4:1-3*

REFLECT In the wilderness, Jesus was tempted to prove himself to, perform for, or please everyone. Who are those wilderness voices in your head—a circle of friends, your parents, your teachers? What do these voices say? Where are you confused about which voice to trust, which path to take? Record your thoughts.

PRAY In Luke, "a voice came from heaven" at the time "when Jesus was praying." Spend a few moments in prayer once again listening to the "voice from heaven." Then ask God for help in any situation where you need to know which voice to trust or which path to follow.

ACT Be sensitive to others who may be struggling with the temptation to listen to "wilderness voices." Find a way to bless them with God's voice through a simple word or action that conveys, "You are God's; you are loved."

WEEK TWO A WILDERNESS JOURNEY

Day 2 Reading

After his baptism, Jesus' newly confirmed identity is put to the test. He is led by the Spirit into the wilderness (see Luke 4). Forty days of fasting. Forty sleepless nights. His journey takes a surprise turn. It is as if the purpose to which he is called, yes, his very identity in God, is challenged. Will he remember who he is in the wilderness—in the face of another voice challenging who he is and what that means?

The wilderness is a place of dryness, of cracked lips, blistered feet, and stomachaches. A lonely landscape of questions and doubts, of deep longing. A dis-comfort zone, where we may forget who we are. In the wilderness we are tested by voices who want to tell us who we are. If we don't know who we are, the world will tell us. And that answer will undoubtedly not match the identity God gives us.

We all face deserts every day. We are surrounded by questions about who we are—from inside and from outside ourselves. In his wilderness experience, we see Jesus remembering who he is by recalling passages of scripture ("One does not live by bread alone" [Luke 4:4]; "It is written, 'Worship the Lord your God, and serve only him'" [Luke 4:8]). We have available to us words of hope and promise from God's Word, words that remind us of who we are in God.

So here's an invitation to you: see this pilgrimage as a challenge to remember each day that you are God's beloved child. That is your true identity. What might it mean to live each day with that knowledge embedded in your heart?

LEARNING TO TRUST

Day 3 Exercise

READ MATTHEW 3:13–4:11.

Then Jesus came from Galilee to John at the Jordan, to be baptized. . . .
Then Jesus was led up by the Spirit into the wilderness.
—Matthew 3:13; 4:1

REFLECT Draw on paper your mental picture of this scripture passage. If the River Jordan represents life and love, what places, people, and practices make up the river of life for you? Draw or write them on your picture.

   If the wilderness represents the testing of Jesus' identity and purpose, what places, people, and ways of living make up your wilderness? Add them to your picture.

PRAY On your drawing, create a stream connecting the river of life with an especially tough place in your wilderness. Through prayer, do the same; ask for God's love and help to flow into that wilderness place in you or your situation. Visualize it happening.

ACT Find a special word or scripture verse that represents what is needed to carve out a channel of love to that tough place. Carry that word with you through the day.

Day 3 Reading

"Is God out to get me?" Have you ever asked yourself that when everything just goes wrong? You're feeling ill. Your essay is overdue. Your family members are crabby with you. You're broke. And your friends treat you as if you have the plague.

Sometimes the desert chooses you. You have no desire to be there. None whatsoever. But you find yourself in the "valley of the shadow of death" (NKJV), as Psalm 23 says. And no visible way out.

Jesus' trial in the desert mirrors the forty-year struggle the people of Israel experienced in the wilderness on their journey from slavery in Egypt to the Promised Land (see the book of Exodus). Hunger gnawed at their guts. God gave them food, and they still complained. The test was whether or not to trust. Time and again, God gave directions, and people disobeyed or complained. And when things got too tough, they happily built their own god and started worshiping it instead.

When faced with temptation in the wilderness, Jesus did what Israel could not. He maintained a firm trust in God and in God's Word. Jesus believed that food would come in God's good time: he needed spiritual food more than bread. When offered the opportunity to worship evil in return for power, Christ held to his knowledge that God was the one true source of all goodness.

There are few shortcuts in our faith journey. Most of us seem to spend a long time traveling in circles. We look at our lives and think, *I haven't changed at all.* Like the Israelites, we might feel that our spiritual journey is a long hike through the wilderness, with no end in sight. We find ourselves asking, *Where is God?*

In these times, we have a companion who has been tested in the desert and remained true to God: Jesus Christ. We can draw from his strength, his peace, his guidance, when tough times come to us. In these times, we are surprised by springs of fresh water and honey-bread for breakfast, as the children of Israel were in the desert. God never leaves us!

GOING WITH THE SPIRIT

Day 4 Exercise

READ LUKE 1:35; 3:21-22; 4:1, 14-21.

The Spirit of the Lord is upon me . . . to bring good news.—Luke 4:18

REFLECT Take a few moments to look up and read these verses in
Luke that refer to the Spirit in Jesus' early life (his birth, baptism, testing,
sending). At these points the Spirit was preparing him for a life of service to
God and people. In what experiences has the Spirit of the Lord prepared
you for service, and in what current circumstances or encounters is the
Spirit preparing you? List them.

Write, "The Spirit of the Lord is upon me to _____." Complete the
sentence in as many ways as you can imagine. What does God have in mind
for you?

PRAY Imagine that the Spirit is like the wind of God and your life is like
a sailboat. If you were to hoist your sail, where would the Spirit lead you to
go? What would the Spirit lead you to do? Ask for help to hoist your sail,
set your rudder, and find out.

ACT Choose one phrase from Luke 4:18-19 that stands out for you. In
response, do one thing today for someone else, led by the Spirit of the Lord.
Record your plan. See what happens and write it down.

Day 4 Reading

The Gospel of Luke tells us that after his baptism and trial in the wilderness, Jesus stood up in his local church and announced his plan for cosmic change. For world peace. For healing. For an end to hunger. A manifesto of freedom—spiritual and even political. So often in his ministry, Jesus quotes the great prophets of old in order to say that right now, God is going to do what has been promised for so long.

And so Jesus reads these remarkable, earth-shaking words from the book of Isaiah: "The Spirit of the Lord is upon me, because he has anointed me to bring good news to the poor . . . release to the captives . . . recovery of sight to the blind . . . to let the oppressed go free, to proclaim the year of the Lord's favor."

Few words in scripture are so charged with purpose. This is no less than the mission statement of the Son of God. Jesus says to them, "These words have come true today!" The air in the synagogue is electric. People stare, mouths open, amazed. They ask, "Is not this Joseph's son?" They wonder, should we follow this teacher?

A blessing. A trial. A mission. This is the start of Jesus' ministry. These are the steps in his call. Love. Test. Purpose. And God's call is in all of them. God's call to Jesus is to be the one he must be. To trust God. To do God's will. Jesus' call is to be God's blessing for the whole world, an endless pouring out of redeeming love for all time.

Jesus' mission, his call, makes the pathway for our pilgrimage. He clears the way ahead. Freedom, justice, wholeness and peace for all—spiritually and physically. Good news. Great news!

HAVING COMPANIONS ON THE WAY

Day 5 Exercise

READ MARK 1:1-20.

In those days Jesus came from Nazareth of Galilee and was baptized by John.—Mark 1:9

REFLECT In the background of Jesus' life are people who prepared the way for him (like John the Baptizer, parents, friends, and the synagogue in Nazareth), as well as people who shared the way with him (like the disciples).

On the five fingers of one hand, name five people who have prepared the way for you on your spiritual pilgrimage. Draw an outline of your hand in your journal. Write these names in the outline of your fingers.

On the five fingers on the other hand, name five who are sharing the way with you now in your group whom you need to get to know better. Jot down their names.

PRAY During the day, when you look at your hands, say a prayer for those who have been, and those who are becoming, an important part of your spiritual life.

ACT Call one person you listed on each hand to say hi, and tell them why you have been thinking about them and praying for them.

Day 5 Reading

You've started a shared journey with your *Way of Pilgrimage* group. Having companions on the pilgrimage makes all the difference in the world. We all need support, encouragement, and guidance from others, and we grow through being able to give something to others.

From the beginning of his ministry Jesus relied on companions. His twelve disciples were just some of those who traveled with him, offered him hospitality, and learned from him. Mary and Martha, Zacchaeus, Nicodemus, Salome, Cleopas, and many others were not only followers but also friends.

Although they called Jesus "teacher" and at times were clearly in awe of him, Jesus was not a distant authority figure. He and his companions walked dusty roads together, slept out under the stars, offered ministry to many people, debated questions of faith, and no doubt laughed a lot. They were even accused of partying too much! Traveling with Jesus helped his friends discover who they really were, as well as who he really was.

It is impossible to make it on any big journey by ourselves. Besides, it's not much fun!

When we lose the will to keep going, or when life stops being enjoyable, it is often because we feel isolated from the people who support us along the way. We are created to live in community.

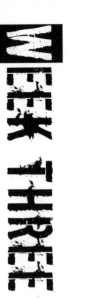

In this week's daily exercises we glimpse the faces of the grace of God—seeking us, accepting us, and growing us up in faith. Open yourself each day to the grace of God already at work in your life. Use your journal to record your thoughts.

SEEKING (PREVENIENT) GRACE

Day 1 Exercise

READ LUKE 15:11-32.

REFLECT Jesus described God's love with a parable of a loving father "who had two sons." The younger of the sons took off on a pilgrimage away from home. When he'd wasted everything, he "came to himself"; he remembered his father and made a return pilgrimage home.

Where do you see yourself in the story of the younger child? Looking back, where do you recognize God's grace seeking you, keeping alive the possibility of change and opening the way?

PRAY Talk with God a bit about where you, like the prodigal son, are beginning "to be in need" (verse 14) or to question the path you are on. Capture your conversation in writing.

ACT Pray for someone today that you're worried about.

Day 1 Reading

Last week we read that Jesus' calling and ministry began at his baptism, where he heard himself named and knew himself as the beloved son of God. Yet the groundwork for Jesus' pilgrimage through life was laid long before this moment. His pilgrimage began in the very heart of God and then, by God's spirit, in all the people who came before him and prepared the way: Mary and Joseph, John the Baptizer, even the wise men and the shepherds.

If we pay attention, we can begin to see that the Holy Spirit's action has likewise prompted every awakening to God on our life's journey. Desmond Tutu, former archbishop of the Anglican church of South Africa, was first attracted to the Christian faith as a nine-year-old growing up in a black township, a disadvantaged area in South Africa. In the 1940s, a white Anglican priest was working among people in that township during the terrible days of apartheid. Tutu's mother was a maid. One day Tutu saw that priest walk past his mother, a black domestic worker, and lift his hat in greeting. Such a simple greeting between a white person and a black person was unheard of. In that moment, Tutu knew there must be something to the Christian faith. His awakening to faith had begun.[1]

Life is pure gift, unrequested and beyond our power. The spiritual life too is offered to us from the heart of God long before we ever become aware of it.

God's grace precedes, follows, surrounds, and sustains us always. It is a constant and consistent gift. We cannot stop it or change it. We are eternally cradled in God's abundant and life-giving grace. This dimension of God's ever-present love has sometimes been called "prevenient grace," literally, the grace that "goes before us."

This week we will explore three dimensions of God's grace: "seeking grace" (God seeks your company), "accepting grace" (God accepts you unconditionally), and "growing grace" (God helps you become more Christlike). The theological terms for these aspects of grace are *prevenient*, *justifying*, and *sanctifying grace*. Don't let the big words scare you away from understanding these gifts God gives us! Grace is the way God shapes and sustains our lives as we move from being strangers to close companions of God. So keep reading and pondering!

ACCEPTING (JUSTIFYING) GRACE

Day 2 Exercise

READ LUKE 15:11-32.

REFLECT Jesus' parable continues, portraying a father who seems almost foolishly in love with his two sons. He eagerly receives and forgives his wayward child because he is so happy the son is returning.

Reflect on the father's response to his younger son's return even "while he was still far off." In what ways have you experienced God's unlimited acceptance and forgiveness of you just as you are, even while you were "still far off" (and maybe smelling like the pigs)? If you have experienced this quality of God's love, you have known "justifying," or saving, grace.

PRAY In prayer, imagine God running toward you to receive you now with welcoming arms. Stay with that prayer image for a while and let God love you just as you are for as long as you can.

ACT Go to someone you've been cut off from. Start over, reconnect, forgive or ask for forgiveness. Let God's acceptance of you spill over!

Day 2 Reading

The Christian idea of grace is rooted in scripture and always reflects God's redeeming love reaching out to us. The Bible tells the story of God's saving work on behalf of all people. This work is always undeserved, yet God tirelessly reaches out with love, acceptance, redemption, covenant community, and companionship to each and all of us without precondition. All we need to do is receive and respond in wholehearted gratitude!

Christians see grace most clearly in God's act of self-giving through Jesus Christ. In the suffering love and forgiveness of the Cross, we see grace in all its fullness. Here is how Melia Warren experienced God's *accepting—justifying—grace* in her life when she was a teenager:

> I truly realized God's accepting grace and felt God's love in a very special way the summer after ninth grade while attending Chrysalis. (Chrysalis is a three-day weekend for young people to discover or rediscover their spiritual self, to realize who they are in Christ.) Over the course of the weekend, I was showered with God's amazing love and grace through challenging speakers, engaging relationships, interactive worship, agape gifts, and other amazing moments.
>
> After the chapel service one evening, we were asked to spend some time in silence. In those moments, I felt God saying to me, "Melia, I love you because you *are*, no strings attached. I desire for you to walk in my grace and allow me to lead you into paths unseen." This at first was scary; I had known about God's love and grace all of my life, but not until that moment had I truly experienced the love which Christ was offering to me. Late that evening, I accepted God's great love and grace for me with no strings attached and said, "God, even though I don't understand everything, I truly surrender all I am to you."
>
> In those moments, I realized that Christ loved me and offered his grace for me regardless. His grace did not depend on anything that I had done or had not done, or any good purposes, desires, or intentions that I had. That weekend my life completely changed.
>
> I am still on this journey that began almost nine years ago.

WEEK THREE GRACE ON THE PILGRIMAGE

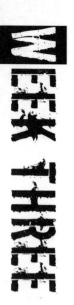

GROWING (SANCTIFYING) GRACE

Day 3 Exercise

READ LUKE 15:11-32 A THIRD TIME WITH ATTENTION TO THE STORY OF THE OLDER BROTHER.

REFLECT Jesus describes an older brother, who, though he stayed home and worked with his father every day, did not share his father's generous and merciful heart. He was far from being at home with the father's love, farther than his returning brother. Outwardly he never left home, but inwardly he was far away.

If you were in this scene, would you respond to the younger son more like the father or the older son? Write how you would respond.
The pilgrimage to life with God means growing to be more like God. Where would Jesus say you are cold or closed and in need of grace to open your heart wider?

PRAY Ask Jesus to help you see the truth about where you are cold and closed to certain people. Pray for grace to open your heart to someone and to let go of fear, hurt, anger, prejudice, jealousy, or whatever gets in the way of that relationship.

ACT Stop and say hi today to someone you typically exclude from your circle. Start a conversation; listen to that person.

Day 3 Reading

There is a natural progression in our experience of God's grace. The Spirit builds on the foundation of justifying grace to help us grow more like Jesus. Becoming Christlike is the work of *growing,* or *sanctifying, grace.* This aspect of grace leads us to bear the fruits of the Spirit (Gal. 5:22-23) and to exercise the gifts of the Spirit (1 Cor. 12:4-11). Growing in grace evokes more questions and helps us understand the challenging life to which Christ calls us. Seventeen-year-old Grant Collier writes about this kind of grace:

> My time at Duke Youth Academy answered many questions but certainly posed more. Knowing that I want to be more Christlike and live into my baptism is a commitment that neither I nor anyone else can ever fully understand. Not only does it take us far beyond the shallow accepted paths of our society but beyond any attempts we could ever make to follow Christ.
>
> I learned that in order to live as a Christian, I must live according to every word of Christ and not a selection of views that I feel can apply to my life within my comfort zone. Christianity is supposed to be hard. If we are to be true followers of Christ, we must take on that full responsibility. As most of us know, Jesus did not live an acceptable, comfortable life according to the standards of the day. He owned very little, had no home, and was under constant pressure. Why? Because he chose not to live the life of comfort and normality but to live a life of service and equality. Jesus didn't simply give what he felt comfortable giving, he gave everything he could possibly give, and this is our challenge as Christian people. We can't expect others to join us in faith if they hear the words but don't see the application. We must show them by our actions so that they might see Christ in us. Living in a society where material things drive us, we must break the bond of want and worry and live as born-again people. When we are baptized we become part of a new story. It is not the story of the kingdom of this world but of the kingdom of God, and to understand that we must understand what we are being called to do.
>
> So, the next time you decide to give in to society's trends, remember that you are different. You are a follower of Christ.

WEEK THREE GRACE ON THE PILGRIMAGE

THE MEANS OF GRACE

Day 4 Exercise

READ LUKE 15:11-32 A FOURTH TIME.

REFLECT The father in this story expresses outwardly what's he's feeling inside. Record all the visible ways the father communicated or signaled his love to each son.

In your pilgrimage, what are the outward expressions of love you've found especially meaningful?

Means of grace are outward ways we can experience and grow in God's welcoming love along the path. What are the means of grace (relationships, spiritual practices, worship, acts of service) through which God seems to draw near you to touch and call you forward in love?

PRAY Be honest with God about ways you have withheld or blocked Christ's love. Offer yourself to be a means of grace today, a vessel of love to someone in particular.

ACT Take a little symbol of God's love with you today as a means of grace for you (perhaps a cross, a special stone, or a devotional booklet or magazine). If you see an opportunity, give it to someone as a means of grace.

Day 4 Reading

Author and speaker Rueben Job tells this story about his childhood, which illustrates the means of grace:

> In my first year of school, I contracted scarlet fever. I became very ill and did not return to school for an entire year. For weeks I was delirious and unable to be out of bed. Then when I became strong enough to sit up, my mother prepared a special place for me to get well. We lived in a modified sod house with walls nearly three feet thick. Each window had a large, boxlike well inside the house, where my mother often kept plants through the winter.
>
> When I was strong enough to sit up, my mother made a little nest of pillows for me in a south-facing window well. Then she carried me from my bed to this place of healing comfort. Perhaps she intuited the healing virtues of sunlight. Certainly, she knew I would be safe, warm, and near to her. While the illness was long and in many ways devastating, one of my happiest childhood memories is being nestled there in the light and warmth of the sun. I could look outside and see my father working. I could see and hear my mother nearby, cooking, mending, and doing what mothers of growing families did.
>
> The winter sunlight, pouring through that south window, warming, giving light and hastening my healing, is for me a wonderful image of God's grace. The gift of grace is always present to give light, warmth, comfort, and healing.[2]

Placing ourselves in a position where we may benefit most from the life-giving light of God's love is the purpose of every means of grace. The means of grace are methods and practices we use to "put ourselves in God's way." They help us become receptive.

The traditional means of grace include worship, the sacraments of baptism and the Lord's Supper, prayer, fasting, scripture reading, and community. Each is a well-tested means to receive and absorb God's life-giving grace.

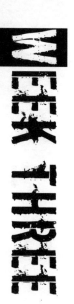

OPENING TO GOD'S GRACE

Day 5 Exercise

READ LUKE 15:11-32 A FIFTH TIME, THINKING ABOUT WHAT MIGHT HAPPEN NEXT AND HOW THIS UNFINISHED STORY WILL END.

REFLECT Jesus leaves the story for us to finish, so do some creative writing. Use your imagination to continue the pilgrimage of each character. What does the father say to the younger son the day after the party about what it means to be back on the family farm? Does the older son ever realize how inwardly distant he is from his family and open his heart to change? Do the sons remain self-centered, or do they grow in loving relationship with their father?

PRAY Ask Jesus to help you see how far or near you are in your heart from the heart of God. Draw a prayer picture of your inner pilgrimage— from your little heart to God's big heart. What are some obstacles God faces in trying to reach you? Where do you need help to open your heart to love?

ACT Call someone in your group and tell each other how you would finish Jesus' story. Then share how each of you, by the grace of God, would like to finish your own stories.

Day 5 Reading

The readings this week have illustrated the "faces" of God's grace: *seeking* (prevenient), *accepting* (justifying), and *growing* (sanctifying). Jesus' parable illustrates all three faces of grace:

Seeking (Prevenient) Grace: "But while he was still far off, his father saw him." While the son was furthest from relationship with the father, even when he had squandered all he'd been given and wallowed in the pig pen of life, the merciful father seems to be standing in the background with eyes of compassion, watching and waiting for him to return home. We are never so far off that God cannot see us and save us. Even the remembrance of God can be a means by which God reaches into us and starts a process of turning us around.

Accepting (Justifying) Grace: The story continues that when the son "was still far off, his father saw him and was filled with compassion; he ran and put his arms around him and kissed him." The father didn't wait for the son to complete his repentance speech ("Father, I have sinned . . .") before he welcomed him home, accepted and forgave him, and restored relations with him without condition. This is the steadfast love with which God accepts and receives us, and gives us a chance to start again.

Growing (Sanctifying) Grace: The father says to the elder brother, "Son, you are always with me, and all that is mine is yours" (verse 31). These words describe an ongoing relationship with the father and an invitation not only to share literal ownership of the outward estate but to share the father's inner life. Likewise, God gives us God's very life in Jesus Christ. Sanctifying grace empowers us to persevere in love and to grow in Christ's likeness.

Just as our lives are unfinished, so the end of this story is unfinished. Once the party was over, what chores needed attending to? What relationships needed mending? We are left to wonder about the conversation that may have happened in that family the next morning at breakfast. How did they continue to grow? And how do we?

This week we are beginning to realize the sacredness of our life journeys so far—in places, people, and time itself. As you think about your own life in relation to the exercises this week, keep your journal close by to jot down ideas; these notes will come in handy for the week's group gathering.

SACRED JOURNEY

Day 1 Exercise

READ MARK 1:14-20.

The time is fulfilled, and the kingdom of God has come near; repent, and believe in the good news.—Mark 1:14

REFLECT Jesus traveled throughout Galilee calling people to wake up to God's presence and the possibilities for transformation so close at hand. When were you first aware of the reality of God? How have you felt the divine presence in the midst of life? Describe your memories.

Think about your picture of what Jesus called the kingdom of God "on earth as it is in heaven"—his vision for the sacred possibility God sets before us in every circumstance of life. Describe or draw an image of what you envision.

PRAY Imagine you can rewind your life and then watch it in fast-forward mode. As you watch your life unfold, give thanks for the holy moments in the course of your journey and for God's presence in all the moments you do not remember.

ACT In all you touch today—people and things, honor Jesus' words: "the kingdom of God is close at hand" (RSV).

Day 1 Reading

When have you experienced the sacred? For some people, *sacred* means "special" or "precious." "Don't touch that! It's sacred to me!" For Christians and Jesus through the ages, *sacred* has often meant "holy"—set apart for a special purpose. The Hebrew people carried the ark of the covenant as a sacred symbol of God's presence with them in the wilderness. People ordained to be ministers or priests were said to be "set apart" for a sacred calling, dedicated to God in a special way. Church buildings often have been described as sacred because they are built for the worship of God.

But think about it. Are churches the only sacred places? What about a serene beach sunset? Are worship services the only sacred times? What about the birth of a baby? Or a parent's word of forgiveness?

If all of creation bears the signs of its Creator, might not all spaces and times have the capacity for sacredness? Might not God be seen and known in surprising places—on the rubble of a garbage dump, in the face of a foreigner, at the eye of the storm, at the last gasp of life?

Brother Lawrence, a seventeenth-century Carmelite monk, described the dishes he washed in his kitchen as sacred vessels that helped to draw him deeper into the presence of God. For him, God's presence might be found everywhere. All of life was a sacred journey.[1] A large part of our pilgrimage involves learning to open our eyes and experience the presence of God around us—to see and treasure the sacredness of all people, of all creation.

SACRED SPACES

Day 2 Exercise

READ MARK 1:14-20.

> *The time is fulfilled, and the kingdom of God has come near; repent, and believe in the good news.—Mark 1:15*

REFLECT Jesus called the disciples by *the Sea of Galilee*, as he stood on the *shoreline*, while Simon and Andrew sat in their *boat*. Ordinary places become sacred spaces when we open to God's presence. And particular places where we experience divine presence become reminders of God's availability to us anywhere.

What ordinary places have become sacred to you because you have experienced God's presence there? To which of these sacred spaces do you return?

PRAY In your imagination, think of an ordinary place where you like to pray. Imagine yourself there, and rest with God for a few moments. Enjoy God's presence with you.

ACT Go to a place today where you have never prayed before. Ask God to make it a sacred place where you can recognize God's presence.

Day 2 Reading

Perhaps God is most easily seen in creation, a mirror to God's awesome power and gentle crafting of our world. And yet, for me, other places have also become holy ground along my pilgrimage.

- two tiny chapels in Boone, North Carolina, with amazing fresco paintings of the Last Supper, and a crucified, risen Christ—and a memory of bread broken and wine shared . . .
- a memorial pool in Port Arthur, Tasmania—the scene of a terrible tragedy and now a place of hushed reflection and prayer, of contemplating the value and fragility of life . . .
- an outdoor labyrinth, a prayer pathway, recently constructed at our college—a place of sweating as we dug and placed brick pavers and then walking the gentle path with God . . .

The sanctuary in my church is also a sacred place for me. Sure, sometimes church seems boring; and although I am sitting there, my mind is somewhere else. Yet as I worship week in and week out, I gather in many holy moments that make this place a reminder of a God who is ever-present yet ever-new. When the building is silent and I am there alone, it still seems thick with the saints of God and the chorus of angels.

Having some places as sacred, as special and set apart, provides me with a reminder that all places are sacred, despite evidence to the contrary. The more we become aware of God's presence in the world, the more each and every place reveals the hand of the One who shaped it.

Pilgrimage is a journey to find the holy every day, in the same way as those who travel to holy places. Being on pilgrimage means choosing to live in the land of the sacred.

WEEK FOUR

THE VIEW FROM THE ROAD

SACRED PEOPLE

Day 3 Exercise

READ MARK 1:17-18.

And Jesus said to them, "Follow me and I will make you fish for people."
And immediately they left their nets and followed him.—Mark 1:17-18

REFLECT Simon and Andrew sensed the sacred in the person Jesus.
When Jesus called, they accepted him *immediately* as their spiritual mentor
and guide for living. Who have been the sacred people—mentors, guides,
and companions on the way for you? With whom have you sensed an
immediate connection and trust?

How does Jesus rate as your spiritual mentor and guide—on a scale
from 1 to 10? Is he more a wise man you have read about or a personal
mentor with whom you have a relationship?

PRAY Jesus sensed the sacred—the divine image—in all people. And he
taught all his disciples to do the same. Think back on all the people you
have encountered in the past twenty-four hours. With the eyes of your
heart, see each person as sacred, and pray for each to be blessed with a new
awareness of God.

ACT See each person today as a sacred child of God.

Day 3 Reading

I did not know it was going to be the worst morning of my life. Mom did not wake me for school as she usually did. I didn't smell breakfast cooking. I knew something was wrong when I walked down the hall to my mother's room and saw that she was still in bed. I walked into her room and sat on the edge of her bed. She turned to me with tears running down her face and told me that he had died. My father, who lived in Seattle, had been diagnosed with terminal cancer earlier that week. He was given six months to live. Now, only days later, my father was gone.

I was sitting in a chair in the living room in absolute silence when the doorbell rang. My youth minister walked in, sat down beside me, put his arm around me, and cried. Throughout that day, others from our church stopped by, stocking our kitchen with meals that would last for weeks. They loved us and cared for us when we could no longer care for ourselves.

There are endless stories like mine of people who have been lifted up and sheltered by the church when their lives came crashing down. Probably you know some of them. Perhaps your story is such a story. When and where have you experienced this kind of care and community?

Community is easy to speak of but often hard to find. In sports, people talk of the team as a family, until a losing season when the coach and lead players are fired. Advertisers promote take-out meals and margarines that will make our homes happy. Politicians promise that if we all work together, we can all be as one, while their policies divide nations and neighborhoods.

All of us look for a place to belong, a safe place to be nurtured and valued, and most of all a place that helps give our lives some meaning. Real community is a true gift from God. German theologian Dietrich Bonhoeffer said Christ is the heart of true community. He said that when we relate to one another in community, it is as if Christ stands between us. The Christ in me sees the Christ in you. And vice versa.[2]

SACRED TIME

Day 4 Exercise

READ MARK 1:16, 20.

> *As Jesus passed along the Sea of Galilee, he saw Simon and his brother Andrew casting a net into the sea—for they were fishermen. . . . Immediately he called them; and they left their father Zebedee in the boat with the hired men, and followed him.—Mark 1:16, 20*

REFLECT Jesus regarded each moment as sacred time, as an opportune time to receive God's presence, to show what's possible, to fulfill human life. Simon and Andrew had cast their nets hundreds of times. Zebedee had spent hours mending his nets. Yet when Jesus called Simon and Andrew in the course of their fishing, an ordinary time became sacred time.

What are the sacred times in your life? Draw a line across a page from left to right and mark the years. Then mark the timeline with memories of points when ordinary times became sacred time for you—when you perceived a time of fulfillment, eternity breaking in, or deep mystery overtaking you, hearing a call, or God drawing near.

PRAY Ask for eyes to recognize sacred moments as they happen.

ACT Set your iPod, cell phone, or digital watch to alert you at each hour. Stop and inwardly notice God in your day.

Day 4 Reading

My uncle came into the living room, put an empty cigar box on the couch, and said it was a gift for me. He asked me to sit down beside him. Then he began telling me what a precious gift life is and that we continually need to be aware of the power of a moment. He invited me to place in this little box items from special moments in my life. It was his way of encouraging me to be aware of the events, people, and times that gave me life.

Sacred time is not clock time. The holy moments in our lives often seem to move in slow motion—sitting with a friend chatting for hours, a long gaze across an awesome canyon, a time of singing and prayer that seems to stretch into eternity, playtime with young children from a poor village on a mission trip to Mexico.

When we experience the sacred, time drips and oozes; minutes seem like hours. The rush of the week is all forgotten. We find ourselves living in the moment, basking in goodness—hyperaware of God's presence. What sacred or holy moments have you experienced lately? When has God's presence overwhelmed you to the point that time seemed to slow down?

It may be that such times just happen without preparation. A jug of blessing, drizzled over us—a slow-motion shower of grace. But perhaps they happen to us less often when we are rushing from one activity to the next, not even noticing today.

We often experience sacred time in sacred places. When we choose to be in a place where we have known grace, our receptiveness to God's presence alongside and within us grows. Holy moments also occur when we are in the company of sacred people. To simply be with someone who is a living saint and everyday angel—whether that person is gardening or visiting a sick person—offers a chance to learn to move to a different rhythm.

Sacred time most often overwhelms us when we have stopped, slowed down, and started paying attention to our inner spirit and to the beauty around us. The closer we travel toward the heart of God, the more our time opens up for moments of grace, revealed and celebrated.

WEEK FOUR

THE VIEW FROM THE ROAD

SACRED STORY

Day 5 Exercise

READ MARK 1:17.

And Jesus said to them, "Follow me and I will make you fish for people."—Mark 1:17

REFLECT The moment that Jesus called out to Simon and Andrew, he began to weave their ordinary lives with his life, their everyday stories with God's story. Their stories became sacred stories the moment they heard the words "Follow me."

How would you tell your sacred story? Can you point to a single encounter, like the one Simon and Andrew had with Jesus, that marks its beginning? Review your journal entries for this week and the previous weeks. As you do so, be thinking about the various ways you could tell or portray your spiritual life story:

- Chart a spiritual timeline
- Draw an image or map
- Write a poem
- Use a biblical metaphor
- Simply write your story

Consider the important experiences, highs and lows, lasting influences, and big "Aha's." Take time to work out how to present your spiritual life story. Then be prepared to share your journey with the group this week in a way that feels comfortable to you. Each person will have ten to fifteen minutes to offer what he or she has chosen to prepare.

PRAY Trace the timeline of your life that you drew in Exercise 4, stopping your finger at each point, giving thanks for God's drawing near to you.

ACT Find someone today with whom you can share at least a small portion of your story.

Day 5 Reading

The Bible brims with stories and symbols of God's presence. Moses knelt before a burning bush, sure that he beheld a clear sign that God was speaking to him, calling him. Later he led the people of Israel into the desert, trusting a pillar of cloud by day and a pillar of fire by night as signs of God's leading. Along their journey, the Hebrew people built the Ark of the Covenant, a holy container representing God's presence among them.

Pilgrims journey to many places. For that reason, through the ages, pilgrims often have carried symbols to remind them not only of home but of who they are—their faith and identity as children of God, as people of the Cross. Symbols have no power in themselves. Instead, they are like chapter headings in a storybook, pointing to an event that has been revealed in a grand narrative. Of course, bread and wine, broken and poured, are more than symbol: they are sacrament; and in the breaking and pouring, eating and drinking, we not only remember Christ, we experience him.

In my own life, a few symbols with strong memories and deep meaning are significant as chapter headings. What symbols, the chapter headings in your faith journey, hold deep meaning for you? How do they remind you of your story and help you to remain connected with God?

This week we look at the obstacles we encounter on pilgrimage. We discover we must let go of some things in order to be ready for pilgrimage. Keep your journal close by to note your thoughts.

SETTING SIGHTS TOO LOW

Day 1 Exercise

READ MATTHEW 5:43-48, PART OF JESUS' SERMON ON THE MOUNT.

REFLECT Setting your sights too low—within easy reach—can keep the journey from truly transforming you and the world around you. Draw an image of a mountain. This mountain represents the God-adventure for which you were born and to which Jesus calls you. On the lower slopes write "loving those who love me." On the middle slopes write "loving those who don't love me or don't know me." On the higher, steeper slopes near the peak write "loving my enemies and praying for those who persecute me." Now at each level write names of persons, groups, or relationships that challenge your ability to love.

PRAY Close your eyes and imagine Jesus inviting you to come join the group that's learning to climb this mountain, offering to help you at each point along the way. What do you say to him? Tell him what assistance you feel you'll need.

Take a moment to lift to God in prayer a challenging person you would encounter at each level of your pilgrimage on the mountain of God's love.

ACT Make a point to encounter someone you prayed for today. Think of yourself as a channel of God's love when you do, and see what happens.

Day 1 Reading

I was relieved to unbuckle the straps and finally drop my pack. Time for a break. Now I could collapse in the soft snow and rest from climbing. Exhausted, I did not want to move another muscle for as long as possible.

But I had barely taken a drink of water when our guide hollered, "We need to get moving again." In a moment my pack was strapped on my back, and we began our climb once more.

Most people begin this climb around midnight. When the sun comes up over the mountain, the snow begins to melt and turn slushy. This condition increases the risk of avalanche and ice fall. It also causes a person to sink into the snow with each step, as opposed to walking on top of its frozen surface. On the journey to the summit, time is crucial and not to be wasted.

And while it is critical to rest during a climb, sitting too long can lead to hypothermia. This medical emergency is marked by a sense of feeling warm and comfortable, so that the person becomes lethargic and doesn't want to move. Without treatment, hypothermia causes an individual to fall asleep and freeze to death.

Our guide knew when we should climb and when we should rest, when the conditions were right for a certain activity and when they were not.

A state of spiritual hypothermia can overcome us when we do nothing to grow spiritually. We become apathetic about our faith, and soon fall asleep to spiritual realities.

Faced with thousands of options about how to spend our time, we can easily be pulled between overactivity and inactivity. Time can easily seem to rule our lives—having too much or too little. We may sense our day is crammed with other people's expectations. At the other extreme, we can easily waste time. How do we keep ourselves from spiritual hypothermia?

WEEK FIVE OBSTACLES TO PILGRIMAGE

UNDERESTIMATING THE CLIMB

Day 2 Exercise

READ MATTHEW 6:1-18, PART OF JESUS' SERMON ON THE MOUNT.

REFLECT Jesus warns us in these verses about a common temptation to all spiritual pilgrims: when we practice outward piety "to be seen," it is like dressing for pilgrimage, telling stories of great spiritual pilgrims, even going through the motions of climbing, while no longer being genuine about the journey upward.

Draw a fresh picture of the mountain from yesterday's exercise. Imagine having three climbing tools in hand: Jesus' willingness to help (prayer), your ability to let go of other things (fasting), and your ability to reach upward or outward in self-giving (almsgiving). Write on your picture one thing you need to do in each of these three areas in order to progress in love from where you are now.

PRAY Ask God for the help you need (prayer), grace to let go of what holds you back (fasting), and love to reach out where called for (almsgiving).

ACT Take a next step today on the pilgrimage of transforming love. Use one of your climbing tools (prayer, fasting, or almsgiving) today.

Day 2 Reading

They set off up the mountain following in the footsteps of others. They set off up the mountain, but they never came back. They loved the idea of climbing the mountain and wearing the gear, but they had not prepared for the actual journey.

There are stories in the news each year about people who have lost their lives or been seriously injured because they underestimated a climb. Mount Hood in Oregon can be climbed in one day from your car to the summit. And because the mountain is easy to get to, as many as sixty people may attempt to reach the summit on a given day during the climbing season. This number of people on the mountain at the same time can be one of the greatest dangers of all.

Many of those people climb Mount Hood with little preparation. They think, *How hard can it be?* and follow a crowd of climbers up the trail. How do they know whether or not they are following the right path? And if they fall, they endanger not only themselves but other climbers as well.

You may have guessed over these few weeks that a pilgrimage can be like a climb, a tough journey with hard choices. You've probably gained a sense of the urgency of good timing. Also of learning what to pack and what to leave behind. Of relying on experienced guides and knowing whom to follow. Of keeping one's footing sure in order to take a new step. Of taking risks and learning to trust.

In a section of the Sermon on the Mount (Matt. 6:1-18) Jesus instructs his disciples on practices for genuine living that prepare them for the climb. He gives them tools for the journey ahead: his own willingness to help (prayer), ability to let go of other things (fasting), and ability to reach upward or outward in self-giving (almsgiving).

On pilgrimage we are not left to climb the mountain by ourselves.

OVERPACKING

Day 3 Exercise

READ MATTHEW 6:19-24.

> *Do not store up for yourselves treasures on earth, where moth and rust consume and where thieves break in and steal; but store up for yourselves treasures in heaven, where neither moth nor rust consumes and where thieves do not break in and steal. For where your treasure is, there your heart will be also.—Matthew 6:19-21*

REFLECT We can't climb the mount of transforming love and also hang out on the lowlands of materialism where most people hunker down. Jesus says we have to choose.

Draw a picture of the mountain of discipleship. Around it, add an image of the lowlands of our consumer culture. Write on it words that represent the "treasures" that most attract you, both "treasures on earth" that draw you to stay in the lowlands and "treasures in heaven" that draw you up the mountain.

PRAY Tell God honestly where you feel torn between living for treasures on earth and treasures in heaven. Ask for the wisdom, faith, or help you need.

ACT As an act of spiritual freedom, turn one earthly treasure from your belongings into a heavenly treasure by giving it away in love to someone who needs it. Or find a symbol of the heavenly treasure you seek.

Day 3 Reading

The last three miles of the trail were awful. The pack straps cut into my shoulders, and my hips felt like they were being crushed between two boulders. I grew increasingly agitated at the weight I was now hauling— the weight I had chosen to carry! All I could picture was my gear spread out on the floor a few days earlier when I was packing for this trip. I remembered telling myself over and over, "I may need that while on the mountain, so I had better take it just in case." Now here I was suffering from the extra weight of the junk that I had not needed on the trip. The worst part is that I did this to myself.

Mountaineering has taught me that it is always better to travel light. The same wisdom holds true in life. We tell ourselves so easily we need more stuff. "If I only had this new thing, my life would be perfect." We try to convince ourselves that things will make us happy, and then complain later when our closet is overflowing with junk! But instead of getting rid of the junk, sometimes we just get a bigger closet!

Just as our time can be consumed by constant activity, our interests can be consumed by the stuff we have and stuff we want. A pilgrim people travel light. Why? Because the farther we travel and the steeper we climb, the more we realize what is essential to carry and what is not.

The danger arises in thinking more about the backpack than the journey itself. On the last miles of my wilderness trip, all I could think about was the weight I was carrying. I missed out on seeing a world of wonder all around because so much unnecessary baggage weighed me down.

We find the sense of who we are and why we travel on this pilgrimage in Christ. Stuff is not our enemy, but if it is not kept under control, it can consume us. Simplicity is an unfamiliar concept in a world addicted to things. Keep it simple.

LACK OF TRUST IN GOD

Day 4 Exercise

READ MATTHEW 6:25-34.

REFLECT Climbing the mount of transforming love doesn't go so well if we don't trust God to care for us along the way. It is hard to move along if we're always stopping to store up stuff or anxiously packing everything we might possibly need for security's sake. What worries surface in you as you contemplate it? Look back at your drawings of ascending the mount of transforming love. What are you afraid of losing or missing out on?

PRAY Take your worries, even those that embarrass you, to the God who cares. Ask Jesus what he meant when he said, "But strive first for the kingdom of God and his righteousness, and all these things will be given to you as well." Record your dialogue: "I said . . .; then he said . . .; I said . . .; then he said . . ."

ACT Do one thing today to act on your commitment to "strive first for the kingdom."

Day 4 Reading

Platforms! Platforms! Platforms! I repeat this again and again inside my mind as I kick each foot into the frighteningly steep snow. Every time the toe of my boot contacts the steep mountain face, I quickly glance down to make sure I am standing on a solid platform. When you know they are the main support keeping you on the mountain, you become very dedicated to the platforms beneath your feet.

Climbing up steep snow faces is not the same as walking up a hill. With each step you must kick deep into the snow and then stomp it down into a firm platform that will hold your weight. Taking a step and committing your weight without first making a solid platform causes the snow underneath you to break away, leaving you incredibly off balance or worse—on your way down!

On a pilgrimage, you can move faster and climb with more confidence when you have something firm to stand on. On level ground, you assume that the ground will hold you, without even thinking about it. But on the mountainside, nothing is as it seems.

When you choose a mountain adventure, you leave behind the safe ground that you have known and trusted. Just as you have moved beyond the faith understanding of your childhood, you may discover this pilgrimage requires you to leave behind some of the solid ground of your faith in order to move to a higher plateau. That higher ground promises a richer experience, a deeper knowledge of God, and more mature attitudes toward others.

COMPARING OURSELVES WITH OTHERS

Day 5 Exercise

READ MATTHEW 7:1–5.

REFLECT

Here Jesus points to one of the greatest pitfalls on the pilgrimage: judging how well or poorly your companions are doing instead of paying attention to the stumbling blocks in your own life. Judging others is just another way we fool ourselves into believing we are more righteous than we are, and results in losing touch with Jesus on our pilgrimage.

Draw two final pictures of the journey on the mountain that include the people in your group at various places. Draw the first picture as if the pilgrimage were a race. Draw the second picture as though it were a team adventure with Jesus leading the way among you. What differences do you see in the way you picture your relationship with one another and with Jesus?

PRAY Write a brief prayer for each group member about your hopes for them. Offer to God what you write for each.

ACT Take a symbol of your prayer and hope for the group, or for each member, to the meeting to give them.

Day 5 Reading

Although I love to climb Mount Hood, it has one of the worst approaches imaginable—a ski run. Many mountains have wild and scenic approach climbs that lead to the really exciting parts of the journey. But on Mount Hood, you get out of your car and immediately find yourself walking uphill next to a ski lift for about two hours. I find this one of the most challenging parts of the climb.

The march up the ski run to get to the real climb is a slow slog— repetitive steps taken endlessly. Boredom and fatigue set in quickly. It seems that this part of the climb will never end. There is little to see except a ski lift that seems to taunt you; you are walking when you could be riding! Mentally, you tell yourself climbing really isn't worth it. The summit is hours away; there is nothing to see; and all you can do is take steps— thousands and thousands of steps!

In the long haul, though, all those little steps will make a difference. But at the start, they are just steps—tedious and tiring.

What steps have you taken so far along this pilgrimage? Make a list of memories or experiences, personal and from the group time. Which of these have seemed eventful and worthwhile? Which have seemed tedious— boring or repetitive?

In our spiritual journey, it can take quite a while to feel that we have made progress. The spectacular views, the spiritual highs, do not come around every day. Nor should they. On the long haul, we sometimes feel pressure to climb harder and higher. "Why is she making more progress?" "How come he seems so spiritual when I don't feel that way at all?" But the pilgrimage is not a competition. We each grow at our own pace.

Last week we looked at what we needed to cast off, and this week we look at what we need to put on in order to be outfitted for pilgrimage. Open your heart to what the Holy Spirit may be saying to you through these exercises. Keep your journal close by to jot down what you notice.

REMEMBERING WHOSE AND WHO YOU ARE

Day 1 Exercise

READ COLOSSIANS 3:12-14.

As God's chosen ones, holy and beloved, clothe yourselves with compassion. . . . Above all, clothe yourselves with love.—Colossians 3:12, 14

REFLECT

Go to a mirror and let it be an occasion to remind yourself whose you are as a member of Christ's body, saying several times: "I am God's chosen one, holy and beloved." Say it with conviction and celebration!

"As God's chosen one," what attitudes have you been wearing that need to come off? What of Christ's character do you need to put on? You are free to select from Christ's entire spiritual wardrobe, beginning with the qualities offered in these verses.

PRAY Let getting dressed for the day, outfitted for sport, or undressing for bed be an occasion in prayer to dress spiritually as well as physically. Take off old attitudes that clothe you, especially those that tend to cling, and give them over to Christ. Receive the new clothes he gives you and, with his help, put them on. Wear them today with dignity.

ACT When you stand before a mirror today, remind yourself, "I am God's chosen one, holy and beloved." Remember whose clothes you are privileged to wear. Today live as Christ would if he were in your place.

Day 1 Reading

In the daily exercise we talk about "letting go" of old attitudes and "putting on" the character of Christ. Another way to visualize this process is to imagine walking a labyrinth. A labyrinth is a circuitous pathway within a circle, created especially for meditative walking.

Since the early centuries of the faith, Christians have used labyrinths for pilgrimage—a time to connect with God while walking a path. The labyrinth offers a path to the center, in which we are invited to shed whatever keeps us from experiencing the heart of God. We reach the center and rest in the love of God. Then we journey out again, putting on the clothing of love as we go out into the world again.

As you walk the labyrinth path, you are conscious of journeying *with* God and also journeying *toward* God. That is what Christian pilgrimage is about.

Along the labyrinth path, all kinds of connections between this prayer walk and your spiritual pilgrimage surface—sometimes as questions like *Where am I heading?* and *What am I trying to achieve?*—but often simply as stirrings in the soul, unspoken promptings of the Spirit.

In my personal experience, arriving at the center of a labyrinth has brought an overwhelming sense of relief, of having climbed a mountain and come to rest in God's presence. I have been able to sit and simply *be* with God.

On the return journey from the center of the labyrinth outward, I often find my heart and soul stirred with thoughts and images of what I am being sent to, of the world in which I live and the discipleship to which I am called, of how I am different because Christ is with me.

Pilgrimage is a journey deeper and deeper into the heart of God. The objective is not getting somewhere or achieving something. Instead, pilgrimage concerns our *being* more than our *doing*. And yet it is not just about being called but also about being sent. May your pilgrimage so far have brought you closer to God's heart!

OUTFITTED FOR PILGRIMAGE

CLOTHED WITH CHRIST'S HUMILITY

Day 2 Exercise

READ COLOSSIANS 3:12-14.

> *As God's chosen ones, holy and beloved, clothe yourselves with compassion. . . . Above all, clothe yourselves with love.—Colossians 3:12, 14*

REFLECT Consider the part of your life of which you are most proud. Name it in your journal. Would you say you wear that part of your life with humility or with arrogance, with gratitude or with an "I deserve it" attitude? What attitude does Christ see?

PRAY If, "as God's chosen one, holy and beloved," you find that you are wearing this part of your life with arrogance or ungratefulness, present it to Christ in prayer for a makeover. Even if your attitude is humble, offer and open further that special part of your life to God. Let Christ enable you to see this dimension of your life as a sacred privilege through which you can respect others "as God's chosen, holy and beloved" and help them discover their own belovedness.

ACT Wearing the humility of Christ, go out of your way to engage in a conversation or activity with a person outside your circle of friends, someone who is not so special in the eyes of your peers. Be as Christ to that individual.

Day 2 Reading

In my junior year in college, I was hired as a residential child-care worker at a children's home. I remember thinking that I finally had a job that mattered! I was tired of selling fast food, washing cars, and doing yard work: I wanted a job to be proud of. At the children's home I could be a professional, and my work would mean something. I had huge hopes and dreams of how I would change the lives of the boys there. Little did I know the lessons that awaited me.

I was assigned to the therapeutic program in Cottage One. When other staff heard where I was working, they gave me certain looks. Cottage One was a small house where up to twelve boys lived at any one time—the place where the most difficult kids ended up. The home took children who had come from very abusive situations and needed closely supervised care.

Soon enough I discovered that instead of changing lives, I was changing wet bedsheets. Instead of having answers to all their problems, I found myself sobbing in the darkness of my room, realizing that I didn't have answers after all. In Cottage One my heart was broken and my faith was tried. And most painful of all, my pride was exposed. Humility became my daily lesson, and I began to discover how to serve.

One of the key lessons on pilgrimage is humility: putting God first and learning to serve others. So much change is going on in your own life that it is natural to focus on yourself. Coping with school, family issues, friendships, part-time work, sports and hobbies, along with the physical and emotional changes in your life, can take up most of your energy. But along the way, God desires to lead you to a realization that the universe is not centered on you. Sometimes you choose the path to humility by taking on serving tasks. Sometimes you learn the hard way that being proud or boastful doesn't earn anyone's respect.

Humility comes from discovering that ultimately, all wisdom, all compassion, and all truth come not from us but from God. The good news is that when we are mindful of God's presence with us, recognizing that all goodness comes from and points toward God comes more easily.

CLOTHED WITH CHRIST'S PATIENCE

Day 3 Exercise

READ COLOSSIANS 3:12-14.

As God's chosen ones, holy and beloved, clothe yourselves with compassion, kindness, humility, meekness, and patience. Bear with one another . . . forgive each other; just as the Lord has forgiven you.—Colossians 3:12-13

REFLECT Draw stick figures to represent the people who most frequently try your patience—in your home, your school, or your church. By each figure, draw a face that reflects your attitude toward the individual, the face he or she would see beneath your surface. By each of these, draw another face that reflects Christ's presence and his attitude toward you both. Take time to imagine Jesus' face, especially his eyes. What do you see?

PRAY As God's chosen one, "holy and beloved," humbly and honestly tell Jesus of your difficulty with each person; tell all that makes you impatient. Receive the grace of Christ's patience and forgiveness for *you*. Let Christ outfit you for offering the same grace to those who try you so much.

ACT Practice wearing the patience and compassion of Christ today when you are around someone who usually tests the grace of God in you. Try to be with that person in the way Jesus would be if he were in your place. As you listen to that person, breathe deeply of Christ's spirit.

Day 3 Reading

He came out of the kitchen in a rage and threw a raw egg at my face. I blocked the first one with my arm, but the second one caught me square in the chest. The egg exploded. Streams of yellow goo wrapped around me and ran down onto the carpet. Immediately after my egg-yolk baptism, the boy showered me with R-rated words of hate. He was quickly restrained.

I had been caring for him for over a year, yet he still had so little respect for me. He treated me this way when he did not get his way or was angry about anything. It was another day at the children's home and another step in my peculiar pilgrimage.

Serving others is easier when they appreciate it. But when they reject your care or throw it back in your face—that truly tests your patience. When you do a kind act for someone and it is rejected, you tend to throw up your hands and say, "It's useless! This person will never change!"

Change always takes time—in the lives of others and in our own. To trust that God is at work despite all signs to the contrary requires patience—one of the fruits of the Spirit. Generally, the more impatient we feel and act, the longer the change ends up taking! Our frustrations get in the way of the transforming work of God's love.

Impatience might not always be a bad thing. To be impatient about ending a war or getting food to hungry people or medical help to the sick can be constructive. More often, however, our impatience means we speak without listening and act without considering the full consequences.

The path of patience involves acting in ways that honor God and trusting that things will work out in God's time. When Jesus tells his followers to pay back evil with good, he is not offering a quick and simple solution to the problem of wrongdoing in the world. Instead, he invites his disciples to take on the character of God, to be clothed in Christ and then to trust a better outcome in the long run.

Have you noticed that people who seem most trusting of God have a "still center"? They are not easily fazed. People like that can be the calm point in the middle of a storm. The patience and hope they display in tough situations comes from a firm trust that God "is working all things together for good" (see Rom. 8:28). Pilgrimage is a path of patience.

LIVING YOUR WORSHIP EVERY DAY IN EVERY WAY

Day 4 Exercise

READ COLOSSIANS 3:12-17.

As God's chosen ones, holy and beloved, clothe yourselves with compassion. . . . And whatever you do, in word or deed, do everything in the name of the Lord Jesus, giving thanks to God the Father through him.
—Colossians 3:12, 17

REFLECT

List three to four activities you did yesterday. Initial each one with either your initials or Jesus' initials, depending on whose character you showed forth or whose glory you were seeking.

PRAY List three to four activities you are doing today. In prayer, offer them each to Christ. Let him help you dress for the occasion, prepare the attitude you will bring to your actions and reactions. As you pray with each activity, let him sign off with his initials.

ACT Perform each of these actions in your day in the name of the Lord Jesus, letting him leave his signature through the manner in which you handle them.

Day 4 Reading

It was a normal day in Cottage One. I had dropped the kids off at school and returned home to do chores. I started with the bathroom. Kneeling down on the floor, I began scrubbing one of the foulest toilets I had ever seen. In the background, a radio was tuned to the local Christian station. The chorus of the song playing kept repeating, "Your steadfast love is better than life."

As I sang along on the chorus, something strange happened. I suddenly became overjoyed about cleaning a toilet. I began seeing this chore as a way to express my praise and love for God. In fact, I wanted that toilet to shine for God's glory! Cleaning the toilet became a time of worship. I moved on from there to the sink and the mirror, then to the laundry and on to the kitchen. I could feel God's pleasure as I meticulously cleaned every inch of that house. That day I truly experienced life as worship!

When have you experienced doing an everyday thing and finding God's presence or purpose in that activity?

It is easy to separate life from worship, to see worship as the "spiritual" times and look at regular life as something that we do in between. What if we were to see worship and life as overlapping completely?

In his letter to the Romans, the apostle Paul says that "worship" involves presenting ourselves as a living offering to God. To worship is to make the whole of your life available for God's purpose, to be aware of God's presence every moment. Every place can become a house of worship; every task can be a sacrifice of praise.

LIVING BY THE RULE OF CHRIST

Day 5 Exercise

READ COLOSSIANS 3:12-17.

And let the peace of Christ rule in your hearts, to which indeed you were called in the one body. And be thankful. . . . sing psalms, hymns, and spiritual songs.—Colossians 3:15-16

REFLECT Looking back over the last few weeks with your pilgrimage group, for what do you give thanks?

As you look ahead to the next few weeks, list a few practices that could help you remind one another:

1. who you are in Christ ("God's chosen, holy and beloved");
2. prepare daily for being as Christ would be in your place ("clothe yourselves with compassion");
3. live by the rule of Christ ("let the peace of Christ rule in your hearts").

PRAY Remember each member of your pilgrim group and give thanks to God for some quality about each one. Write down what you give thanks for. Sing a song of praise to God.

ACT Take any one practice you named in your reflection time above and, as an act of gratitude for your pilgrim group, act on it in the name of the Lord Jesus.

Day 5 Reading

Every day at 4:00 PM the door to the cottage flew open and nine boys ranging from the ages of eight to fourteen rushed into the house. They arrived desperate for attention and usually picking on one another. I would spend the first hour calming them down, breaking up fights, and trying to bring order out of chaos. Paperwork, medications, fights, restraints, cooking, cleaning, homework, tantrums: from the time they came in the door until the time they went to bed, I was constantly on my toes. Rest was not an option.

I had taken the job at the children's home confident that I would be able to handle whatever would come my way. As I began to grow increasingly tired of the pressure of working, the initial fire of faith dwindled. When my solutions failed and I realized that there was no spiritual quick fix for our children, my passion started to fade. Work became much harder, and I lost my desire to be there. My spiritual tank was empty; I had nothing left to give.

My spiritual guide asked whether I was keeping a balance between my inward devotional life and my outward life of service. I had never thought about that before, and when I did I realized my internal devotional life was almost nonexistent! I had been trying to serve and do great things for God but wasn't spending focused time each day with God.

There is a rhythm to pilgrimage. In one way it is as simple as breathing. Breathe in. Breathe out. Receive so you can give. Stop to recharge your batteries so that you can continue to be a shining flashlight!

In *The Godbearing Life*, authors Kenda Creasy Dean and Ron Foster say that when Moses encountered the burning bush, the miracle was not that the bush was burning. The miracle was that the bush burned without burning up! Plenty of pilgrims burn themselves out trying to do good for others. That is not what Christ calls us to do. He calls us to live in close relationship with him so that we might constantly be filled with his presence.

Dean and Foster say that when people see a life that is like a burning bush, giving a bright light but not being consumed, they turn and take notice. They ask, "How can this be?" The answer is that God—the "I Am" of yesterday, today, and tomorrow—is present in the bush, giving power and defying destruction.[1]

NOTES

WEEK ONE

1. Robert Frost, "The Road Not Taken," in *The Poetry of Robert Frost,* ed. Edward Connery Latham (Holt, Rinehart & Winston, 1979), 105.

2. From the "Lorica," or "St. Patrick's Breastplate," trans. Cecil Frances Alexander, as quoted in "Patrick of Ireland," by James E. Kiefer (http://justus.anglican .org/resources/bio/124.html).

3. C. S. Lewis, *The Lion, the Witch, and the Wardrobe* (London: Fontana, 1950), 75.

WEEK THREE

1. "Defining Moments: Desmond Tutu," on BBC News World Edition, July 9, 2003, http://news.bbc.co.uk/2/hi/africa/3052274.stm.

2. Adapted from Rueben P. Job, "The Nature of Grace" in *Companions in Christ Participant's Book* (Nashville, Tenn.: Upper Room Books, 2001), 36.

WEEK FOUR

1. See Brother Lawrence, *The Practice of the Presence of God,* trans. Robert J. Edmonson (Orleans, Mass.: Paraclete Press, 1985). Brother Lawrence was a lay Carmelite of the seventeenth century whose writings on "practicing God's presence" have been cherished by Christians of all traditions through the centuries.

2. Dietrich Bonhoeffer said, "Without Christ there is discord between God and man and between man and man. Christ became the Mediator and made peace with God and among men." *Life Together* (San Francisco: HarperSanFrancisco, 1978), 23.

WEEK SIX

1. Kenda Creasy Dean and Ron Foster, *The Godbearing Life: The Art of Soul Tending for Youth Ministry* (Nashville, Tenn.: Upper Room Books, 1998), 72.

JOURNAL PAGE

JOURNAL PAGE

JOURNAL PAGE

JOURNAL PAGE

JOURNAL PAGE

JOURNAL PAGE

JOURNAL PAGE

JOURNAL PAGE